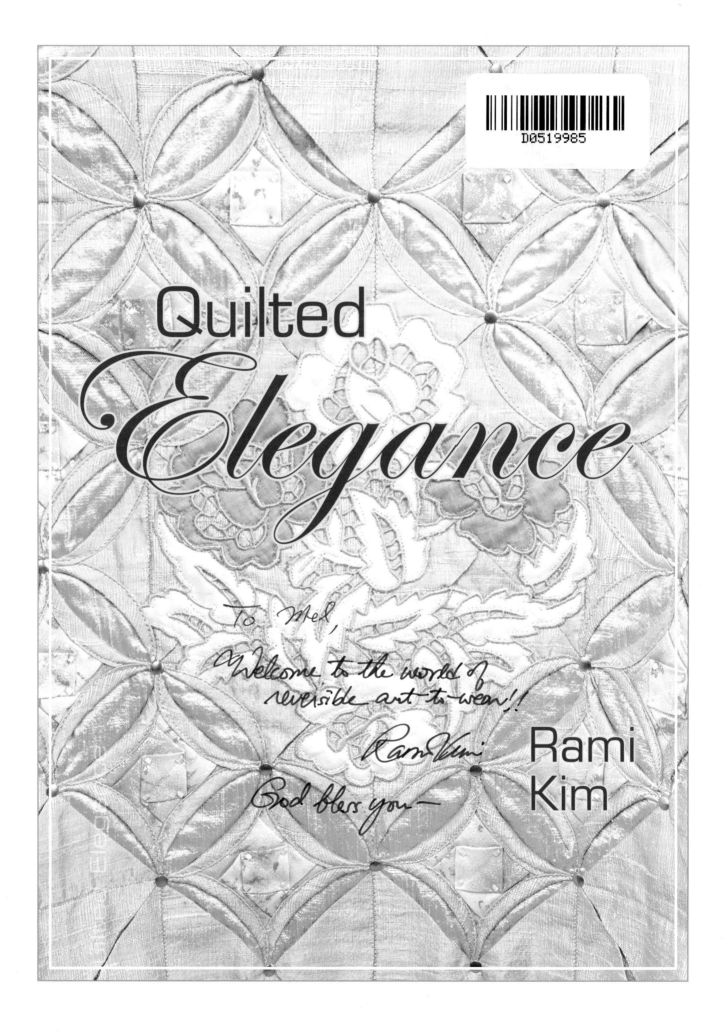

Quilted
Elegance

To Mel,

Welcome to the world of
reversible art-to-wear!!

Rami Kim

God bless you—

Rami
Kim

Located in Paducah, Kentucky, the American Quilter's Society (AQS) is dedicated to promoting the accomplishments of today's quilters. Through its publications and events, AQS strives to honor today's quiltmakers and their work and to inspire future creativity and innovation in quiltmaking.

EXECUTIVE EDITOR: ANDI MILAM REYNOLDS
TECHNICAL EDITOR: MARCELLE CASHON
SENIOR EDITOR: LINDA BAXTER LASCO
GRAPHIC DESIGN: ELAINE WILSON
COVER DESIGN: MICHAEL BUCKINGHAM
PHOTOGRAPHY: CHARLES R. LYNCH
ADDITIONAL PHOTOGRAPHY BY WOOIL KIM
FASHION SKETCHES BY JIYOUNG YUN
ILLUSTRATIONS BY RAMI KIM

Additional copies of this book may be ordered from the American Quilter's Society, PO Box 3290, Paducah, KY 42002-3290, or online at www.AmericanQuilter.com.

Text © 2009, Author, Rami Kim
Artwork © 2009, American Quilter's Society

Library of Congress Cataloging-in-Publication Data

Kim, Rami.
    Quilted elegance / by Rami Kim.
       p. cm.
    ISBN 978-1-57432-978-0
    1. Patchwork--Patterns. 2. Quilting--Patterns. I. Title.

TT835.K48867 2009
746.46'041--dc22
                          2009000916

American Quilter's Society
P. O. Box 3290 • Paducah, KY 42002-3290
www.AmericanQuilter.com

Proudly printed and bound in the United States of America

This book is dedicated to my loving husband, Ken Lee, and my two sweet daughters, Deanna and Chelsey Lee. Thank you, guys, for your love.

Contents

My Personal Letter of THANKS

I naively assumed that writing my second book would be easier than writing the first one. How wrong I was!

During this strenuous but fun-filled process, I am once again indebted to my family, friends, and the members of my church for their love and support. Even though the names are too numerous to mention here, you all know I am talking about YOU and how much I appreciate your help and cherish your never-waning interest to see my second book become a reality. Thanks to YOU, I can dream and make new creations without feeling limited.

Among many sources from whom I received excellent assistance, I would like to acknowledge the wonderful publishing staff of the American Quilter's Society for their gracious help and advice on creating this book. I would like to mention Hobbs Bonded Fibers for supplying the best batting for my works, and Bernina USA for providing my favorite sewing machines once again. Lastly, I want to thank my photographer Wooil Kim, who took breathtaking photos of my works, and Jiyoung Yun for the beautiful fashion illustrations.

Thank you, Lord, for leading me to this fun path of creating and playing with my dreams. I know I am merely your instrument.

Rami
01/01/2009

The Artist's View

My philosophy is that "Simplicity Is the Easiest Way to Achieve Elegance."

In this book, I intended to create art pieces that have more relevance to the life we live today. Quilts were designed to be converted into seasonal wall-hangings. All the jackets and vests are designed to be reversible, with a dressy look emphasized on one side and the other side showing a more casual look. This will be indeed useful on air travel these days where only one luggage piece is allowed to be checked in since a single reversible jacket can function as two garments. Several bag designs in this book have the same "two-sided" concept that allows you turn the bag to display the side that matches a jacket.

When I was growing up in South Korea, I discovered Cathedral Window blocks in Bojahgy, the Korean wrapping cloth, and fold & stack octagonal star block patterns in bolster pillowcases. It gives me great pleasure to create pieces that I can wear or use in interior design using those patterns. It is so wonderful to relive parts of my childhood memories by doing what I enjoy most as an adult.

How to Use This Book

In this book, technique chapters are separated from project chapters to enable you to become accustomed to and master the instructions before starting a project that uses the techniques.

I recommend you try to make a small sample of each technique to get a taste of it. You could even test how color combinations look.

For jacket and vest patterns, it is wise to make a trial pattern in your size to check the fit before you place so much exquisite work on them. Patterns are found on the included CD.

Use this book as a reference of techniques. I hope you can create your own masterpiece to showcase your skills and taste.

Technique A:
Weaving with Wrapped Strips

Preparing the Wrapped Strips

To make a sample weaving strip, cut one 1¼" x 15" strip from a main fabric.

)1¼"

Cut two 1" x 15" strips from an accent fabric.

1"

1"

Stitch an accent strip to the main fabric strip with a ¼" seam allowance, right sides together, aligning the raw edges.

Press the seam allowance toward the accent strip.

Press the accent strip around the seam allowance to wrap the raw edge of the main strip.

¼"

Repeat the same procedure to encase the other raw edge.

Prepare as many 1¼" wrapped strips of the length required for your pattern.

Weaving the Wrapped Strips

Cut a piece of lightweight fusible interfacing 1" larger on all sides of the pattern piece.

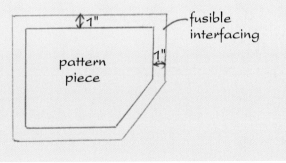

1"

1"

fusible interfacing

pattern piece

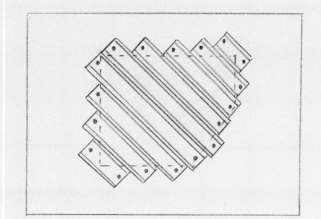

Place the fusible interfacing with the fusible side up on a padded surface.

Lay wrapped strips edge-to-edge at a 45-degree angle on the fusible interfacing and pin to the padded surface.

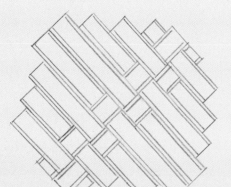

Weave wrapped strips using a simple basket weave (one over, one under) removing and reinserting pins as necessary. Pin all ends down.

When the weaving is done, press woven strips with a dry iron and a pressing cloth to fuse the strips to the interfacing. Allow the piece to cool.

woven piece

pattern piece

Remove the pins. Carefully move the woven piece and place the pattern piece on top of the woven side. Mark the finished line. Stitch on this marked line before cutting off the excess. When you trim, cut outside the stitching line to prevent the woven piece from coming apart.

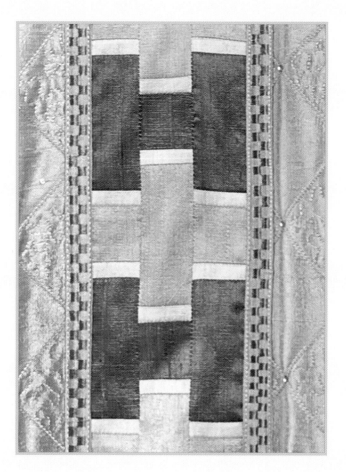

Technique B:
'H' Piecing
('H' is for Happiness)

To make a sample, you need three different fabrics (dark, light, and an accent fabric).

This sample will make a 16" long H panel.

Add 3" to the set 1 cut strip length and 1½" to the set 2 strip length for each additional 4" in length you need for your panel.

For set 1, cut:
 1 strip 3" x 16" of the dark fabric
 1 strip 1½" x 16" of the light fabric
 2 strips ¾" x 16" of the accent

Join the strips with a ¼" seam allowance as shown. Press the seams open.

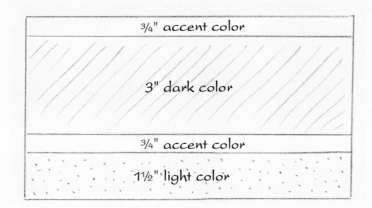

Cut eight 1½" wide segments.

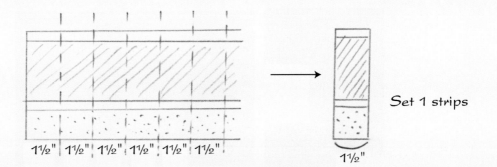

Join the segments into two ribbons as shown, using a ¼" seam allowance.

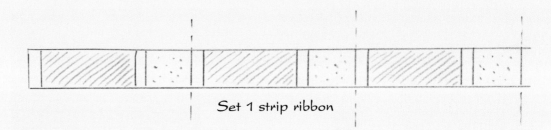

For set 2, cut:

1 strip 1½" x 8" of the dark fabric

1 strip 3" x 8" of the light fabric

2 strips ¾" x 8" of the accent

Join the strips with a ¼" seam allowance as shown. Press the seams open.

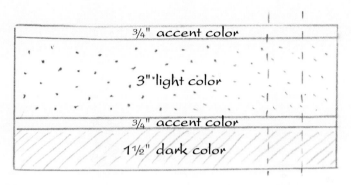

Cut five 1½" wide segments.

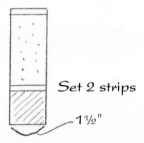

Join the segments into a ribbon as shown, using a ¼" seam allowance.

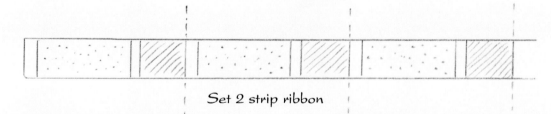

Construct the H by placing the set 2 ribbon between the two set 1 ribbons as shown. Stitch together using a ¼" seam allowance. Press the seams open.

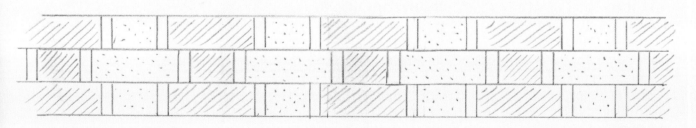

Technique C:
Decorative Stitch Ribbon

Cut a 1⅛" strip of fabric the length needed for your pattern.

Fold in half lengthwise, wrong sides together, by bringing the raw edges together as shown.

folded 1⅛" strip

Position to cover raw edges or randomly to add a decorative accent.

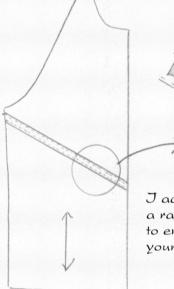

Cover the raw edges with folded 1⅛" strip and edgestitch.

I added decorative stitches with a rayon thread from my machine to embellish more (it is like creating your own decorative ribbon trim).

Add decorative stitching through all layers along the length of the ribbon strip.

Debonair
Jacket & Vest

Debonair
Jacket & Vest

Approximate Yardage Requirements

2 yards light blue

2 yards violet purple

1½ yards sage green

Trace the jacket pattern pieces in your size onto pattern paper.

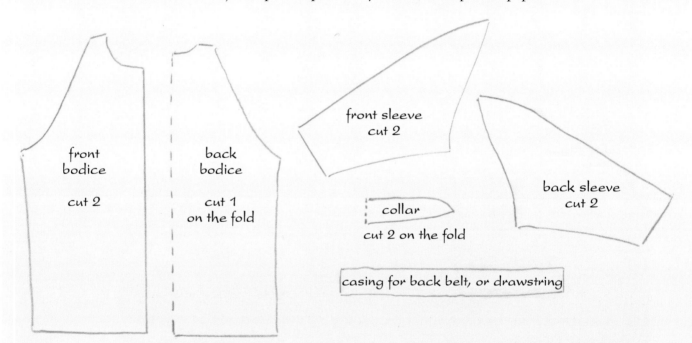

Cut bases for 8 pieces (2 fronts, 1 back, 2 front sleeves, 2 back sleeves, and 1 collar; you don't need a base for the belt casing) from a lightweight batting. I used Hobbs Thermore. Cut the bases 1" larger than the pattern pieces all the way around. You need this allowance since fabric draws up when quilted and stitched.

Draw lines on the front bodice pieces for placement of woven and pin-tuck sections as shown.

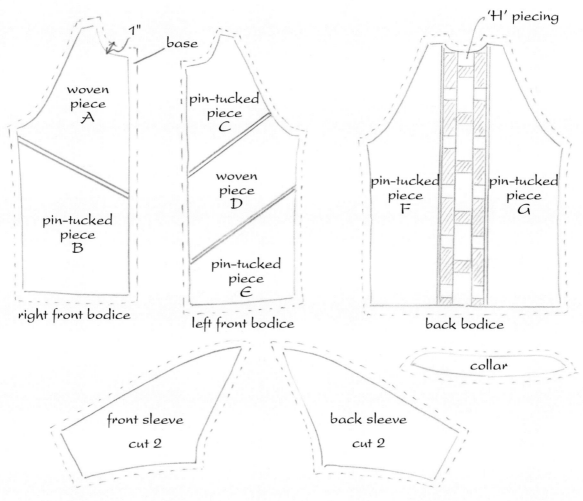

Trace woven piece A and woven piece D sections on separate pattern paper and cut out. Label them A and D. Cut out lightweight fusible web (I used Misty Fuse™ Fusible Web) 1" larger than the pattern pieces.

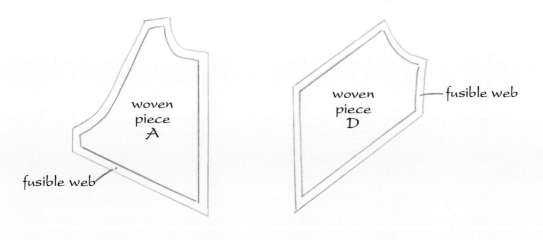

Place front bases on a padded surface and lay the fusible web on top.

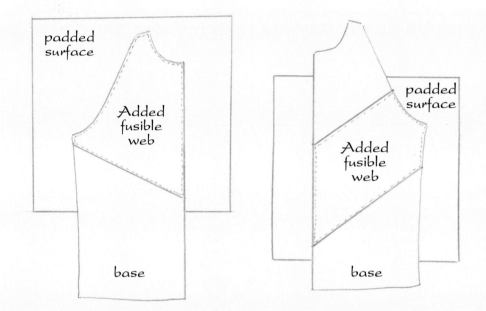

Prepare wrapped strips for weaving. If you use silk dupioni, cut your strips following the lengthwise grain to prevent raveling.

Cut 1¼" wide strips to for a total of approximately 300" of both purple and light blue fabrics.

Cut twice as many strips 1" wide of sage green for a total of approximately 600".

Wrap the purple and light blue strips with the sage green strips according to the Technique A instructions (pages 10–12).

On piece A, place the wrapped light blue strips first, edge to edge, at a 45-degree angle as shown.

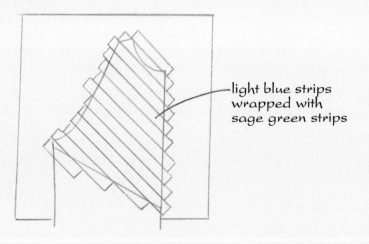

light blue strips wrapped with sage green strips

On piece D, place the wrapped purple strips first, edge to edge, at a 45-degree angle as shown.

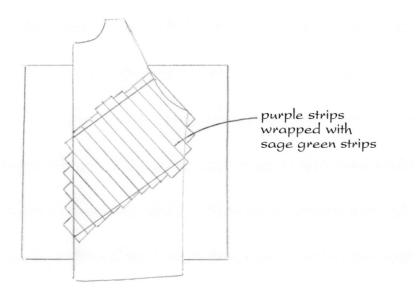

purple strips
wrapped with
sage green strips

Weave and fuse the alternate color strips according to the Technique A instructions (pages 10–12). Use a pressing cloth.

Fuse the woven pieces to the base pieces and trim off excess strip ends even with the edges of front bodice bases.

Quilt through all layers by stitching along the middle of each strip with invisible or decorative thread.

For the right front bodice, cut light blue fabric to cover the remaining base (piece B). Hand-baste onto the base.

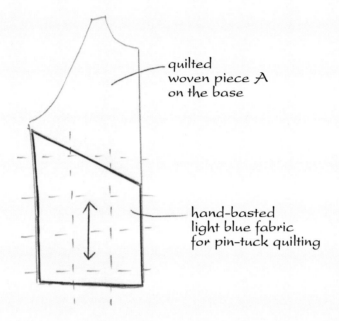

quilted
woven piece A
on the base

hand-basted
light blue fabric
for pin-tuck quilting

Using a size 1.6/80 twin needle, quilt through the light blue fabric and the base following the diagram to create a 2" grid on the diagonal. If you wish, add free-motion stippling in a checkerboard arrangement as shown.

I use a Clover Chaco Liner to mark on silk dupioni. You could also use a water-soluble marker or a quilting guide attached to your machine foot.

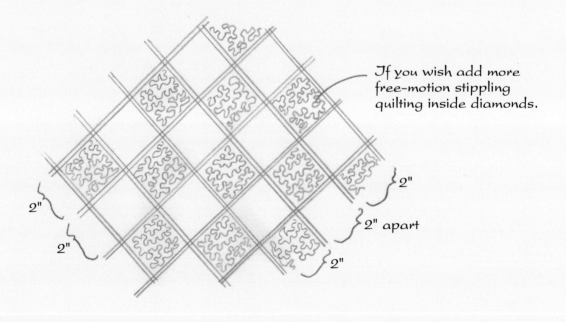

If you wish add more
free-motion stippling
quilting inside diamonds.

2"

2"

2"

2"

2" apart

2"

Cover the raw edge of the woven piece A and pin-tucked bottom piece B with a 1⅛" light blue strip folded in half lengthwise (see Technique C instructions, pages 16–17).

) folded 1⅛" strip

Topstitch in place with a straight stitch. Add decorative stitches with rayon thread.

In the same way, cut blue and purple pieces for the C and E sections of the left front bodice. Baste in place. Quilt through both layers with a twin needle, creating a 2" grid. Cover the raw edges with a folded strip.

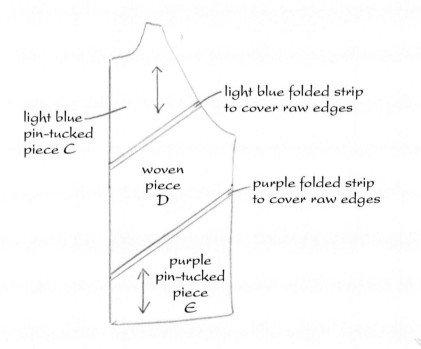

light blue pin-tucked piece C

light blue folded strip to cover raw edges

woven piece D

purple folded strip to cover raw edges

purple pin-tucked piece E

Cut purple fabric for all 4 sleeve bases and baste in place. Quilt through both layers with a twin needle, creating a 1½" grid. Add stippling in a checkerboard arrangement.

1½" apart

1½"

Cut light blue fabric for the collar and baste onto its base. Quilt through both layers with a twin needle creating a 1" grid. Add stippling in a checkerboard arrangement.

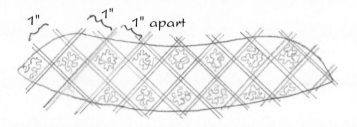

Prepare an H piece for the center of the back bodice following the instructions for Technique B (pages 13–15). The set 1 strips should be cut twice the length of the set 2 strips.

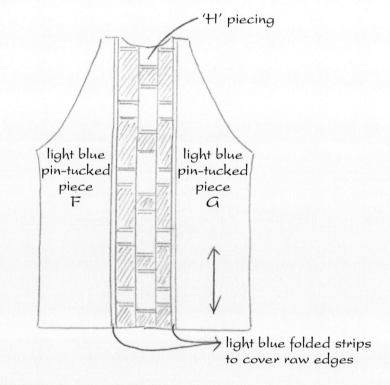

For set 1, cut:

    1 strip 3" x 32" of purple fabric

    1 strip 1½" x 32" of light blue fabric

    2 strips ¾" x 32" of sage green fabric

For set 2, cut:

  1 strip 1½" x 16" of purple fabric

  1 strip 3" x 16" of light blue fabric

  2 strips ¾" x 16" of sage green

Center and baste the H panel on the back bodice base.

Cut pieces F and G from light blue fabric and place on the back bodice base. Baste in place. Quilt through both layers using a 1.6/80 twin needle, creating a 2" grid on the diagonal. Add free-motion stippling in a checkerboard arrangement.

Cover the raw edges between the F, H, and G sections with a folded 1⅛" strip of light blue fabric.

Trim the excess seam allowance from the front bodices, the back bodice, the 4 sleeve sections, and collar using the pattern pieces as a guide.

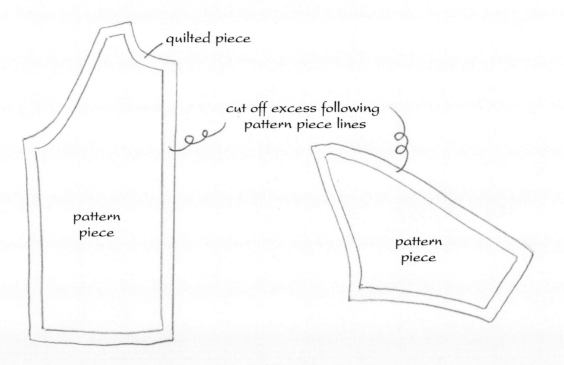

quilted piece

cut off excess following
pattern piece lines

pattern
piece

pattern
piece

Jacket Construction

Stitch the front sleeves to the front bodices, right sides together at the raglan seams, using a ½" seam allowance. Clip the curves and press the seams open.

Stitch the back sleeves to the back bodice in the same manner. Clip and press the seams open.

Place the fronts onto the back with right sides together. Stitch the shoulder and upper sleeve seams matching the raglan seams. Press the seams open.

Add a wrapped strip (from the woven panel strips) around the sleeves approximately 2¼" from the finished length. Position it so that when the underarm seam is sewn, the edges of the strip will match. Topstitch in place.

Stitch the fronts to the back at the side seams and underarm seams with a ½" seam allowance, matching the sleeve seam lines. Press seams open.

Center the collar along the neck edge, right sides together, and join with a ½" seam allowance. Press the seam toward the collar.

Make the lining with the same pattern pieces. In the sample, the lining is the CHELSEA jacket (page 38).

Insert the lining into the jacket with wrong sides together.

Machine baste the outer jacket and the lining together ⅝" from the raw edges all the way around the bodices, collar, hem, and sleeve hems.

Trim off ½" from the raw edge.

Cut 2¼" bias strips and join on the diagonal to form one continuous strip. Press the seams open.

⅝"

cutting line

½" (seam allowance)

The sample jacket used approximately 170" of bias binding, include the binding around the sleeves.

Fold the binding strip in half lengthwise, wrong sides together, and press. Bind the jacket and sleeve edges, finishing to ¼".

Adding a Casing

For a gathered back waist, cut a 2½" wide strip of fabric for a drawstring casing the desired length. Choose to extend across only the back bodice or around to the front bodices.

Fold in the raw edges ¼", press, and stitch onto the lining side through all layers.

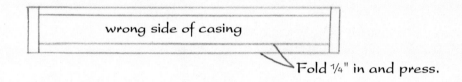

wrong side of casing

Fold ¼" in and press.

Stitch the wrong side of the casing onto the right side of the jacket about 1" below the waistline or on the lining side if you wish to hide the casing. Topstitch both long edges in place.

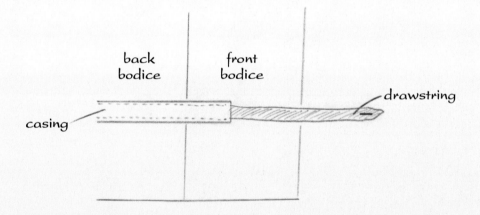

back bodice

front bodice

drawstring

casing

Prepare a drawstring the length of the gathered area with buttonholes at both ends. Stitch a decorative button to the jacket at both ends of the casing.

Insert the drawstring and button to secure in place.

Debonair
Vest

Trace pattern pieces in your size.

Cut bases of lightweight batting for all the pieces 1" larger around all sides.

Follow the same directions used for the jacket to create the right front woven bodice. The sample vest used approximately 150" each of purple and light blue wrapped strips.

Layer the left front bodice and the back bodice silk on the bases, adding the silk organza on top.

Cut 1⅛" strips of sage green silk dupioni and fold in half lengthwise, with the raw edges meeting in the back. The sample vest used approximately 220" of strips.

Place these folded strips on the silk organza in a random criss-cross arrangement.

Top stitch the strips in place with decorative or invisible thread. Add decorative stitching with rayon threads to create the ribbon-trim look.

Join the shoulder and side seams.

Cut a lining using the same vest pattern pieces and join at the shoulder and side seams with a ½" seam allowance.

Insert the lining and machine baste the outer vest and the lining (wrong sides together) ⅝" from the raw edges all the way around the bodices and armholes. Trim off ½" from the raw edge.

The sample vest used approximately 150" of bias binding, include the binding around the armholes.

Cut 2¼" bias strips and join on the diagonal to form one continuous strip. Press the seams open.

Fold in half lengthwise, wrong sides together, and press. Bind the vest and armhole edges. (The finished width of the binding is ¼".)

Technique D:
Fold & Stack Octagonal Star Medallion

When I was young, my grandmother taught me how to create this fold & stack star from paper. Korean people love to put these medallions on the ends of bolster pillows to add texture.

Approximate Fabric Requirements

4–6 different fabrics, ¼–½ yard each

On pattern paper, draw a circle the size of your choice (7", 8", 9" …).

Cut one piece of fusible interfacing using the circle pattern.

On the fusible side of the interfacing, draw lines dividing it into eighths.

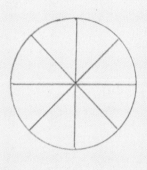

Row 1

Cut five 2½" diameter circles from fabric A.

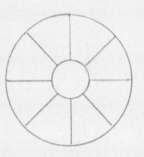

Fuse one 2½" circle onto the center of the interfacing circle.

Fold the remaining 4 circles in half, wrong sides together.

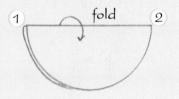

Fold corners 1 & 2 to the center to make a triangular shape.

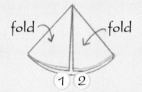

Place the points of these 4 triangles at the center of the interfacing, lining up the center fold and edges with the marked lines. Tack the triangle points by hand stitching a seed bead ¼" from the point through all layers including the interfacing. Hand baste the outer edges in place.

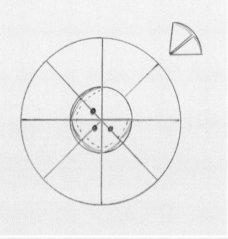

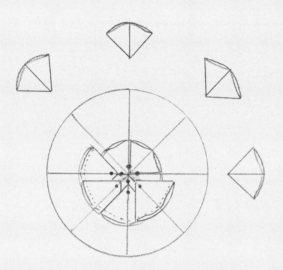

Row 2:

Cut eight 3¼" circles from fabric B and fold the same way.

Arrange the points of the 8 triangles ⅜"–½" from the center of the circle, lining up the center fold with the marked lines.

Overlap each piece in the same direction.

Tack the points through all layers with a seed bead and baste the outer edges in place.

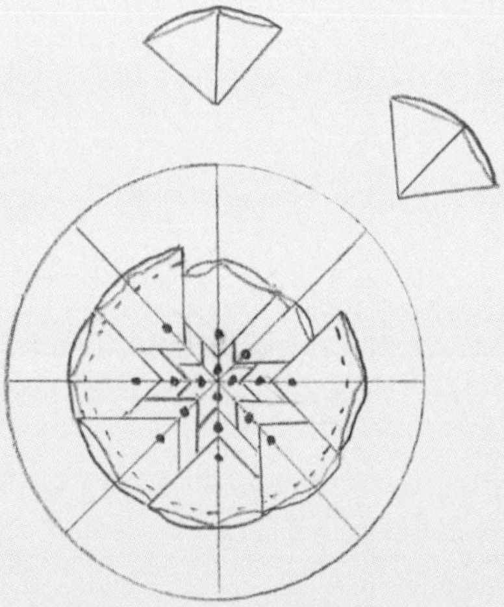

Row 3 and subsequent rows:

Cut 8 progressively larger circles (see the following table) from the next fabric and fold into triangles.

Arrange around the center as before, tacking the points with seed beads and basting the outer edges in place.

Row	Circle diameter	Number of circles
1	2½"	5
2	3¼"	8
3	4½"	8
4	5¾"	8
5	7"	8
6	8¼"	8
7	8¾"	8

Seven rows will make a 13" diameter finished star medallion.

With the last row in place, hand baste ⅛" in from the edge of the interfacing and trim off the excess fabric even with the edge of the interfacing.

Press to fuse to the interfacing.

Cut a 1¼" bias strip the length of the circumference* of the circle plus ½" seam allowance. Stitch the two short ends using a ¼" seam allowance. Press seams open.

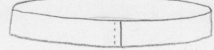

* To calculate the circumference of a circle, multiply its diameter by 3.14.

With right sides together stitch the bias strip onto the medallion with a ¼" seam allowance.

Wrap the raw edge with the stitched bias strip and press under. Topstitch in the ditch with invisible thread through all layers to fix the bias strip in place.

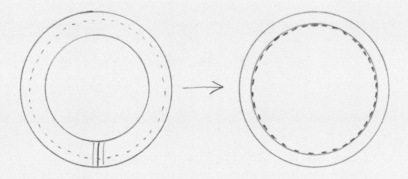

Stitch the medallion onto the background fabric with invisible thread, a walking foot, and a blind or narrow zigzag stitch. Test the stitching on sample fabrics before you stitch your project.

Chelsea
Jacket

Jiyoung Yun

PHOTO: Wooil Kim

Chelsea
Jacket

The CHELSEA jacket is the reverse side of the DEBONAIR jacket. Since DEBONAIR is quilted with a thin batting, eliminate the batting from the CHELSEA jacket to reduce bulkiness.

If you make the CHELSEA jacket as a stand-alone jacket, you will need to add batting and a lining. Refer to the DEBONAIR jacket instructions (page 18–31).

Piecing the Background

Cut light blue cotton strips the width of your fabric as follows:

3 strips 4" wide
2 strips 5" wide
1 strip 6" wide

Cut lavender cotton strips the width of your fabric as follows:

1 strip 1½" wide
2 strips 2" wide
2 strips 2½" wide

For larger sizes, you may need to make a second strip-set.

Make a strip-set using a ¼" seam allowance, alternating colors and widths as shown (page 41). Press the seams open.

Cut into segments 2" and 3" wide.

	3"	2"	3"	2"	3"	2"	3"	2"	3"
4" light blue (LB)									
2" violet purple (VP)									
6" LB									
1½" VP									
4" LB									
2½" VP									
5" LB									
2" VP									
4" LB									
2½" VP									
5" LB									

Cut 1¼" x 35" sage green strips to insert between the segments (number of strips to be cut depends on your size).

Arrange strips alternating pieced strips and sage green strips to create your own background fabric. Join with a ¼" seam allowance.

Place your bodice and back pattern pieces on the pieced background and cut out the shapes 1" larger than pattern pieces on all sides.

Embellish with braided trim or folded strips with decorative stitching (pages 16–17).

Cut sleeve pieces and a collar 1" larger than pattern pieces with light blue cotton and embellish with folded strips.

Make two 7" fold & stack octagonal star medallions. Sew one on the left bodice and the other on the right sleeve with invisible or matching thread using a blind or zigzag stitch.

Construct the jacket following the instructions on pages 18–31.

Insert the CHELSEA jacket into the DEBONAIR jacket with wrong sides together.

Machine baste the jackets together ⅝" from the raw edges all the way around the bodices, collar, hem, and sleeve hems.

Trim off ½" from the raw edge.

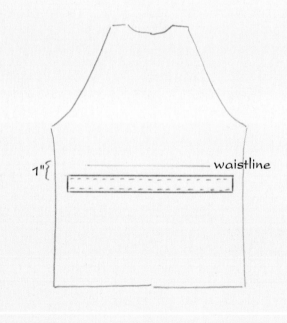

Cut 2½" bias strips and join on the diagonal to form one continuous strip. Press the seams open.

The sample CHELSEA/DEBONAIR jacket used approximately 170" of bias binding, including the binding around the sleeves.

For a gathered back waist, prepare a casing and stitch onto the CHELSEA side through all layers (see page 30).

Debonair/Chelsea
Bag

Making the DEBONAIR Side

Approximate Yardage Requirements
¼ yard violet purple
¼ yard light blue
½ yard sage green

Notions
25" long zipper
½ yard fusible interfacing
½ yard medium loft batting

Using the bag front pattern piece, cut out medium-weight fusible interfacing, adding 1" all the way around.

Place the interfacing with the fusible side up on the padded surface.

Prepare the wrapped strips following the Technique A instructions (pages 10–12).

The sample bag used approximately 130" each of purple and light blue wrapped strips.

Follow the Technique A instructions (pages 10–12) to make the woven bag front.

Making the CHELSEA Side

Cut a medium-weight fusible interfacing and a background fabric 1" larger than the front and bottom pattern pieces.

Fuse the wrong side of the background to the interfacing. Place one layer of medium-loft batting underneath.

Cut 1⅛" strips and fold in half lengthwise, bringing the raw edges to the center back.

The sample bag used approximately 130" of folded strips.

Place the folded strips randomly on the front and bottom backgrounds (see the photos here and on page 39).

Quilt through all layers by topstitching the folded strips in place. Add decorative stitching.

Make one 7" fold & stack octagonal star medallion following Technique D (pages 34–37). Position on the bag front and sew in place with invisible or matching thread with a blind or zigzag stitch.

Constructing the Bag

Press under a ½" seam allowance along the top of both bag fronts.

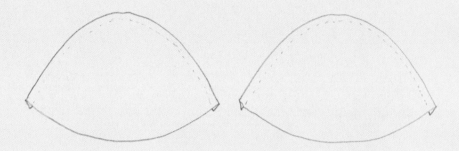

Pin a zipper between two folded top edges and topstitch right next to the folded edges. (It's easier to sew if you open the zipper first.)

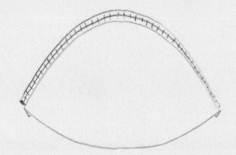

Open the zipper and stitch the bottom piece to the two fronts, right sides together, using a ½" seam allowance. Turn right side out through the zipper opening and press.

Cut 2 fronts and one bottom for the lining. Join the 3 pieces in the same way. Press under a ½" seam allowance along the top.

Insert the lining inside the bag, wrong sides together, and hand stitch the lining to the bag along the zipper.

Install the handles.

Woven Bamboo Forest &

Ethereal Stars Reversible Wallhanging

38" x 44", made by the author

Woven Bamboo Forest & Ethereal Stars

Reversible Wallhanging

Approximate Yardage Requirements for
Woven Bamboo Forest

1 yard light brown

1 yard dark brown

1¼ yards green

1 yard orange-red

1 yard ivory

scraps of greens, reds, gold, and browns

Approximate Yardage Requirements for Ethereal Stars

½ yard ivory

½ yard violet

½ yard beige-gold

½ yard light green

½ yard light blue

4–6 assorted fabrics for the octagonal folded stars, ¼–½ yard each

Notions

10 decorator buttons (5 for each side of the wallhanging)

pattern paper for master pattern

iron-on crystals

Woven Bamboo Forest

Make a master pattern following the diagram.

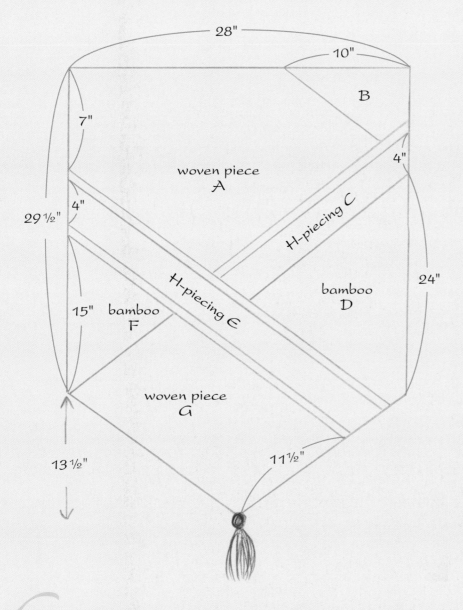

C Cut Hobbs Thermore batting 1" larger than the quilt master pattern all the way around. This serves as a quilt base.

I chose this thin batting since it adds less bulkiness and is easy to quilt.

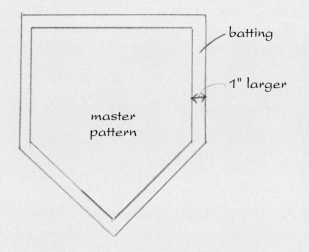

batting

1" larger

master
pattern

Trace the A–G sections onto tracing paper and cut out to make patterns for each section. Add ¼" seam allowance where seams exist and add 1" allowance on outside edges of the quilt. (See pages 71–72 for examples of adding the extra allowance.)

Woven Sections A and G

Using traced pattern pieces A and G, cut lightweight fusible interfacing 1" larger around the edges.

You'll need approximately 240" wrapped strips for section A and approximately 280" for section G.

For section A, cut:

8 strips 1¼" wide of dark brown

8 strips 1¼" wide of light brown

32 strips 1" wide of light green

For section G, cut:

8 strips 1¼" wide of dark brown

8 strips 1¼" wide of light brown

32 strips 1" wide of orange-red

Follow Technique A instructions for weaving with wrapped strips (pages 10–12).

H-Pieced Sections C and E

For section C, set 1, cut:

1 strip 3" x 28" of dark brown

1 strip 1½" x 28" of light brown

2 strips ¾" x 28" of orange-red

Make a strip-set as shown. Cut into 16 segments 1½" wide.

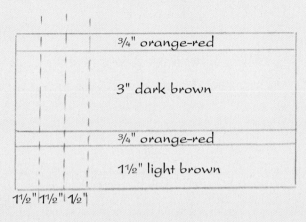

For section C, set 2, cut:

1 strip 3" x 15" of light brown

1 strip 1½" x 15" of dark brown

2 strips ¾" x 15" of orange-red

Make a strip-set as shown. Cut into 9 segments 1½" wide.

Join the segments into ribbons and join the ribbons into an H-pieced section following the Technique B instructions (pages 13–15).

Cut 1 strip 1½" wide of ivory fabric and stitch to the left side of the H-pieced section C using a ¼" seam allowance. Press the seam allowance toward the ivory strips.

For section E, set 1, cut:

    1 strip 3" x 34" of light brown

    1 strip 1½" x 34" of dark brown

    2 strips ¾" x 34" in light green

Make a strip-set as shown. Cut into 20 segments 1½" wide.

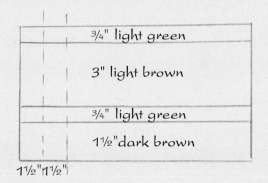

For section E, set 2, cut:

    1 strip 3" x 18" of light brown

    1 strip 1½" x 18" of dark brown

    2 strips ¾" x 18" of light green

Make a strip-set as shown. Cut into 11 segments 1½" wide.

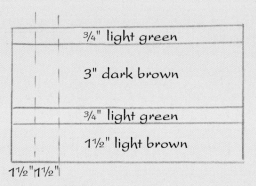

Join the segments into ribbons and join the ribbons into an H-pieced section following the Technique B instructions (pages 13–15).

Cut 2 strips 1½" wide of ivory fabric and stitch to both sides of H-pieced section E using a ¼" seam allowance. Press the seam allowance toward the ivory strips.

Bamboo Tree Appliqué Sections D and F

Cut ivory background fabric 1" larger than the D and F pattern pieces.

Prepare fabrics for bamboo leaves by adding fusible web (Steam-a-Seam or Wonder-Under) to the wrong side of the fabrics. You need dark brown, dark green, light green, gold, and orange-red fabrics for the leaves.

Trace bamboo stems and leaves onto tracing paper, noting the color numbers, and cut out (color key on the patterns). Place the traced pattern pieces on the right side of the appropriate web-fused fabrics according to the color key.

Fuse bamboo stems and leaves in place on backgrounds, following the place-ment shown in the patterns. Satin stitch the raw edges with matching color rayon threads (either 40- or 30-weight).

Full size patterns on CD

Test your zigzag stitch on samples. Lower the top tension of your machine so the bobbin thread does not show on the top. Use tear-away stabilizer under the background fabric to prevent puckering.

Reduce the width of the zigzag stitch gradually as you approach the points of the leaves. Pivot and start increasing the width of the stitch gradually as you stitch away from the point.

Pieces that lie beneath other pieces should be stitched first. When the satin stitching is finished, remove the tear-away stabilizer from the back of the piece. Press with a steam iron to set the stitches into the fabric.

Trim off excess background fabric using the pattern piece.

Cut out section B with light green fabric.

Join the sections in the order shown with a ¼" seam allowance.

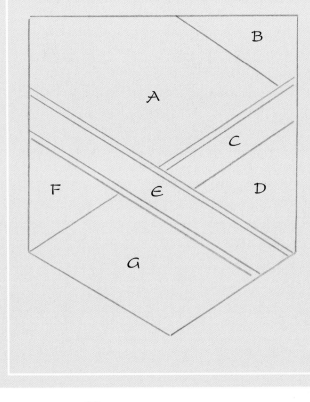

A & B
C & D
A/B & C/D
F & G
E and F/G
A/B/C/D & E/F/G

Quilt the top with the base batting only. Do not add a backing since you are making a two-sided quilt.

Woven Bamboo Forest &
Ethereal Stars
Reversible Wallhanging
38" x 44", made by the author

Ethereal Stars

See page 48 for yardage requirements.

Making the Background

The background is pieced using assorted pale fabrics in light green, violet light blue, and ivory.

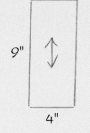

Cut 27 rectangles 4" x 9" in assorted colors.

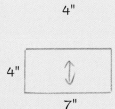

Cut 26 squares 4" x 4" in assorted colors.

Cut 12 rectangles 4" x 7" in assorted colors.

Stitch 3 rows of nine 4" x 9" rectangles on the long sides using a ¼" seam allowance. Press seams open.

Join 5 rows of 4" x 4" and 4" x 7" pieces, in different arrangements of alternating colors and shapes, using ¼" seam allowance. Press the seams open.

Stitch one row of three 4" x 4" squares using ¼" seam allowance. Press seams open.

Arrange the rows as shown and sew together.

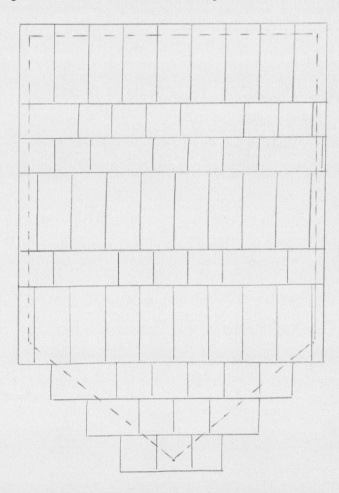

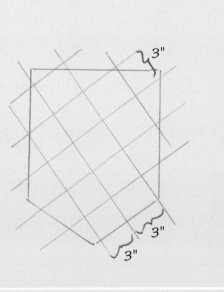

Place batting underneath the pieced background and quilt with a walking foot.

Using the master pattern, mark the outline of the quilt on the right side of the quilted background.

Making the Fold & Stack Octagonal Star Medallions

Cut 5 lightweight fusible interfacing circles in 5 different sizes.

Star	Diameter
a.	7"
b.	8½"
c.	11"
d.	11¾"
e.	13"

Follow Technique D instructions to make the stars (pages 34–37).

Bind the edges of the medallions using 1¼" bias strips.

Star	Length of Bias Binding
a.	22½"
b.	27⅛"
c.	35"
d.	37⅜"
e.	41¼"

Position the medallions on the quilted background as shown and stitch in place with invisible or matching thread and a blind or zigzag stitch.

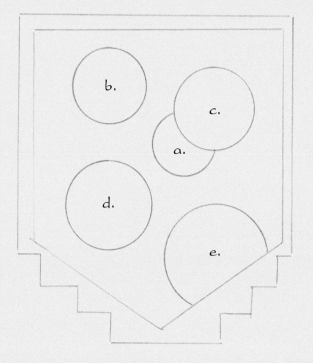

Cut out some lace motifs and stitch to the background in the same way.

Joining the Panels

Place the panels wrong sides together matching the trimmed Woven Bamboo Forest edges with the marked edge lines on Ethereal Stars.

Trim excess off Ethereal Stars.

Machine baste the two quilt tops together by stitching ⅛" from the raw edges.

Cut approximately 130" of 3" wide straight-of-grain strips. Join with 45-degree seams and press the seams open. Fold in half lengthwise, press, and use to bind the raw edges of the wallhanging with a ⅜" seam allowance.

Add iron-on crystals and other embellishments as desired.

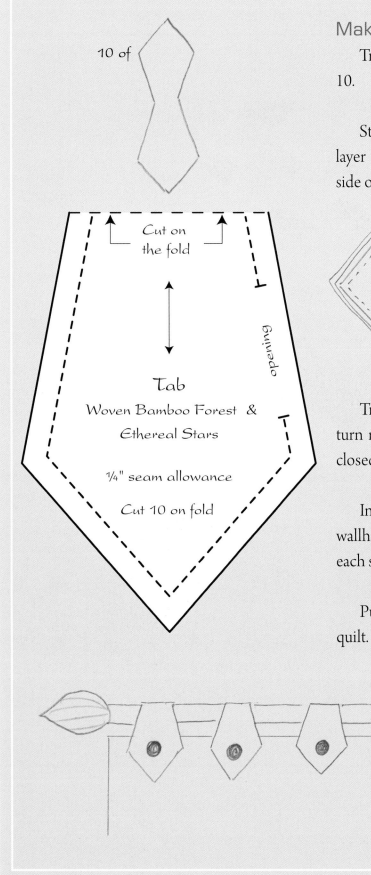

10 of

Cut on
the fold

opening

Tab
Woven Bamboo Forest &
Ethereal Stars

¼" seam allowance

Cut 10 on fold

Making Hanging Tabs

Trace the tab pattern. Place on a fold and cut 10.

Stitch 2 tab pieces right sides together with one layer of batting, leaving an opening to turn right side out.

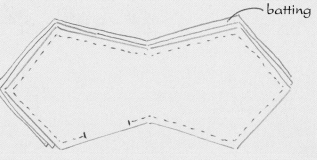

batting

Trim the corners, clip the inside corner, and turn right side out. Press. Slipstitch the openings closed. Topstitch ⅛" from the edge.

Install the tabs evenly across the top of the wallhanging securing them with 10 buttons (5 on each side).

Purchase an elegant rod to hang this two-sided quilt.

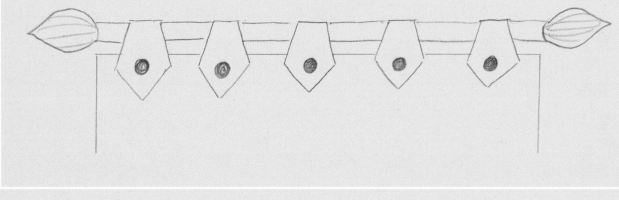

Pillows
with Woven Strips

Yardage Requirements
These pillows were made with silk dupioni.

Materials
Yardage Requirements for pillow 1:
- ¼ yard fuchsia
- ¼ yard orange-red
- ⅛ yard yellow-gold
- 1 fat quarter for backing

Yardage Requirements for pillow 2:
- ¼ yard teal
- ⅛ yard purple
- ⅜ yard yellow-green
- 1 fat quarter for backing

Notions
- 2 purchased 13" x 19" pillow forms
- ½ yard fusible interfacing

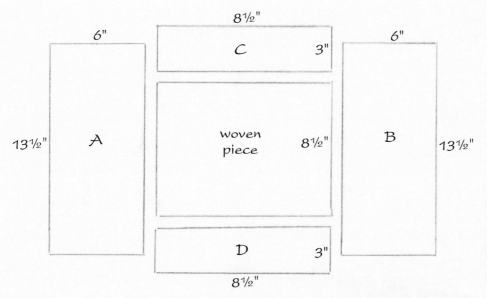

The cut dimensions of each section are shown.

For the center woven section, cut:
2 strips 1¼" wide of fuchsia
2 strips 1¼" wide of orange-red
4 strips 1" wide of yellow-gold

Prepare wrapped strips to the Technique A instructions (pages 10–12).

Weave, fuse, and quilt to a 9" x 9" square of batting. Trim to measure 8½" x 8½".

Cut 2 rectangles 6" x 13½" of orange-red.

Cut 2 rectangles 3" x 8½" of fuchsia.

Fuse interfacing to the backs of the 4 rectangles to add more body.

Join the woven piece with the C and D rectangles, right sides together, with a ¼" seam allowance. Press the seam allowance away from the woven piece.

Add the A and B rectangles.

Cut a back piece 19½" x 13½" and fuse interfacing to the wrong side.

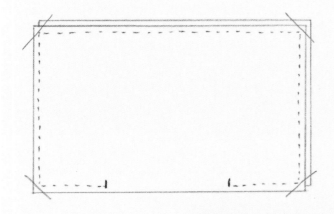

With right sides together, stitch the front and back, right sides together, with a ¼" seam allowance, leaving a 13" opening.

Trim off the excess fabric at the corners. Turn right side out and press.

Insert a pillow form and slipstitch the opening closed.

Make the second pillow in the same way, cutting as follows:
2 strips 1¼" wide of teal
2 strips 1¼" wide of purple
4 strips 1" wide of yellow-green

Cut 2 rectangles 6" x 13½" of yellow-green.

Cut 2 rectangles 3" x 8½" of teal.

Cut a back panel 13½" x 19½".

PHOTO: Wooil Kim

Indigo Denim & French Country
Jacket

Jiyoung Yun

I borrowed piecing designs from a Bojahgy, Korean wrapping cloth, for this jacket. Ancient Korean ladies hand stitched Bojahgy in silks or cottons and used Bojahgy as tote bags. No batting or base is used in this jacket.

Indigo Denim & French Country
Jacket

Approximate Yardage Requirements

1¼ yards main blue denim fabric

¾ yards denim print for sleeves and patchwork

assorted fat quarters in pink, blue-gray, and light blue

Notions

pattern paper

4–6 buttons for INDIGO DENIM jacket

4–6 buttons for the FRENCH COUNTRY jacket

2 buttons for the FRENCH COUNTRY pockets

Trace the jacket fronts and back onto pattern paper.

Draw in the design lines following the diagrams (pages 69–70), arranging and changing them as you wish.

Making Checkerboard Units.

Cut 2 strips 1½" x 18" of fabric 1

Cut 1 strip 1½" x 18" of fabric 2

Make a strip-set as shown and cut into 11 segments 1½" wide.

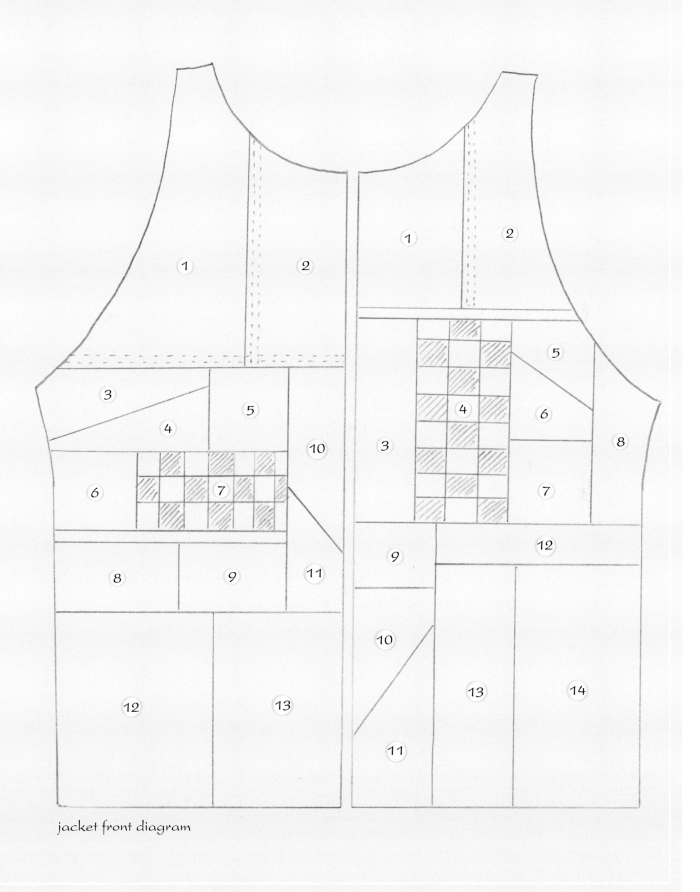

jacket front diagram

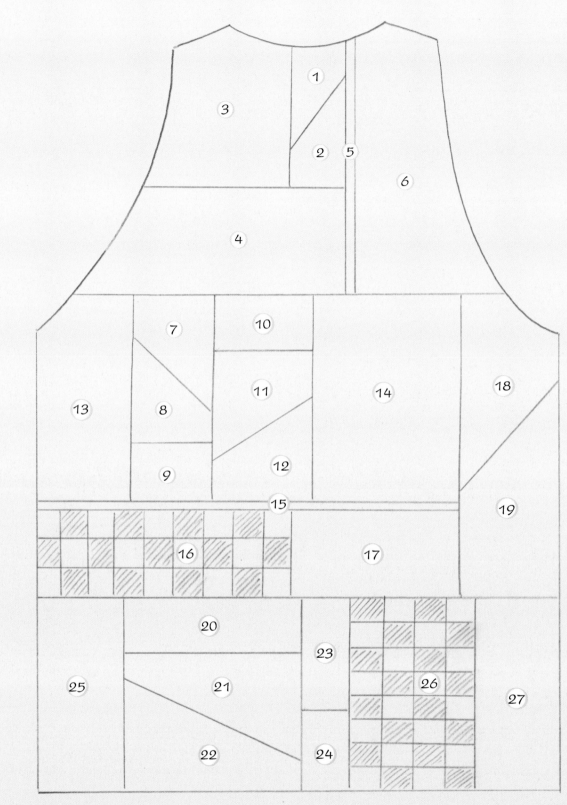

jacket back diagram

Cut 2 strips 1½" x 21" of fabric 2

Cut 1 strip 1½" x 21" of fabric 1

Make a strip-set as shown and cut into 13 segments 1½" wide.

Use the segments to make 3 checkerboard units as shown.

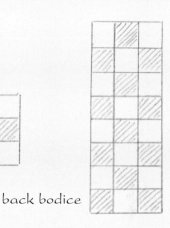

right front bodice   left front bodice

back bodice

Cut 2 strips 1½" x 13" of fabric 1

Cut 2 strips 1½" x 13" of fabric 2

Make a strip-set as shown and cut into 8 segments 1½" wide.

Use the segments to make a checkerboard unit as shown.

Trace each pattern section onto tracing paper and label. Cut them out to use as templates.

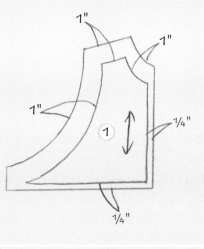

back bodice

Place a paper template on the right side of the fabric. Cut out the sections using a variety of fabrics, adding ¼" seam allowance where they will be seamed and 1" along the outside edges.

For example, section 1 of right front bodice will be traced like this.

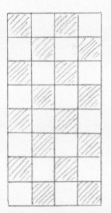

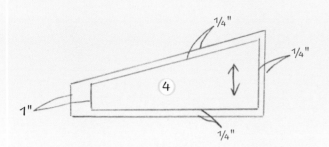

Section 4 of the right front bodice will be traced like this.

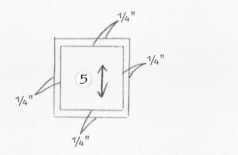

Section 5 of the right front bodice will be traced like this.

Stitch the sections together in the numbered sequence shown on the drawings using a ¼" seam allowance.

Add double topstitching to embellish. Use the pattern to trim off the excess.

Cut the front and back sleeves.

I used two different fabrics for the front and back sleeves to add more interest. Allow an extra 1⅞" in the length to accommodate the hem and elastic casing finish.

Construct the jacket following the directions on pages 28–30.

For a reversible lining, use the same pattern pieces and an interesting patterned fabric. I used a French-style toile and added an accent fabric for collar and pockets.

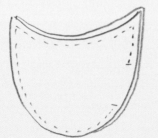

For the pockets, cut 2 in the accent fabric and 2 linings (pattern on CD).

Stitch the accent and lining fabrics right sides together, leaving a 2" opening.

Turn right side out through the opening and slip-stitch the opening closed.

Gather the center 2" in along the top edge and embellish with a button.

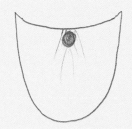

Stitch pockets onto the jacket.

Join the two jackets, right sides together, starting from the back bodice hem and going all the way around, leaving an opening to turn right side out. Do not stitch the sleeve hems.

Turn the jackets right side out and slipstitch the opening closed.

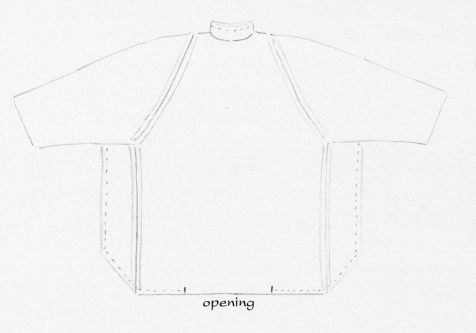

opening

For a gathered waist, cut a 2" strip and press under ¼" all around the edges to make a casing for a drawstring. Stitch a casing 1" lower than your waistline and insert a drawstring. Pull to gather.

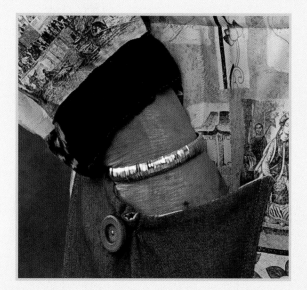

Finishing Up the Sleeve Hems

Fold under a ½" hem on each jacket sleeve. Slipstitch the folded edges together.

Fold a 1⅜" hem toward the FRENCH COUNTRY side to make a casing.

Topstitch the hem, leaving an opening. Insert a 1" wide elastic. Adjust to a comfortable length, join the ends, and complete the topstitching on the hem.

Indigo Bag

utilizing Catheral Window blocks (page 95)

Resonance & Mellifluence

Reversible Apron Vest

Jiyoung Yun

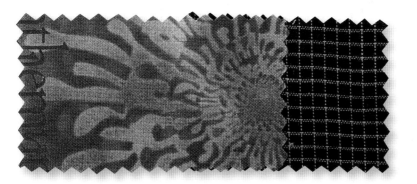

PHOTO: Wooil Kim

Resonance & Mellifluence

Reversible Apron Vest

Resonance Apron Vest

Preparing the Fabric

The cutting measurement and the number of strips needed depends on your size.

Approximate Yardage Requirements

½ yard black plaid
⅜–½ yard red-beige plaid
⅜–½ yard red-orange

Cut:

2" x 24"–28" strips of black plaid
2" x 24"–28" strips of red-beige plaid
1¾" x 24"–28" strips of red-orange

Join the strips with a ¼" seam allowance, alternating the 3 colors as follows.

Stitch a black plaid strip to a red-beige plaid strip, right sides together, matching edges on one side. Use a ¼" seam allowance. Press seams toward the red-beige plaid strip.

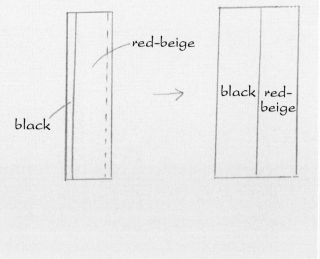

black

red-beige

black | red-beige

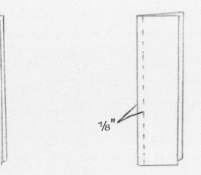

Press again along the stitched seam with wrong sides together.

Stitch a ⅛" tuck.

Press the tuck toward the red-beige plaid strip.

Add an orange-red strip next to the red-beige plaid strip and repeat the same steps as above, pressing the tuck in the same direction as the first tuck.

Continue in this manner until you have pieced enough strips to cover the apron vest pattern.

Mark horizontal lines 1½" apart and stitch across the tucks in alternating directions as shown. Use a walking foot.

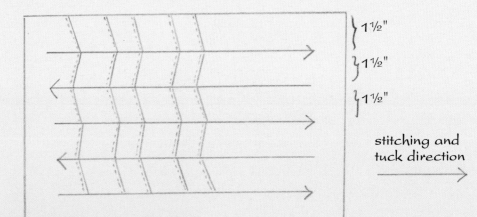

1½"

1½"

1½"

stitching and
tuck direction

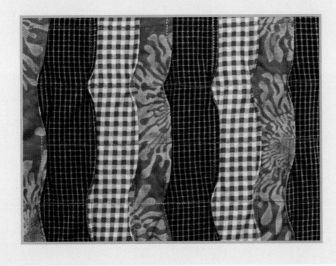

Gently steam press the whole piece. Do not move the iron back and forth.

Constructing the Vest

Cut out one bodice piece from your pieced fabric.

Cut out one reversible bodice lining piece from your other pieced fabric. The sample vest has the MELLIFLUENCE vest on the reverse side (pages 82–86).

Stitch the vest and lining following the diagram, right sides together, with a ½" seam allowance. Trim away excess seam allowance and clip the curves.

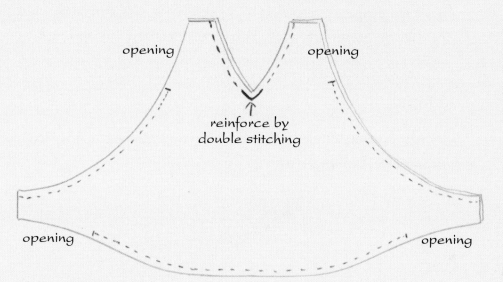

Turn right side out through one side opening. Press.

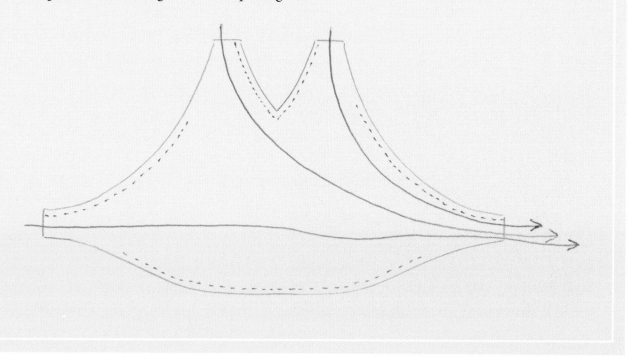

Cut out back straps using the back strap pattern piece. Cut out 2 black print and 2 in black plaid straps.

Stitch one black print piece to a black plaid one as shown below. Repeat.

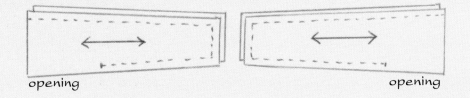

Trim the corners and seam allowance. Turn right sides out through an opening and press.

Cut neck strap pieces on the bias using the neck strap pattern piece. Cut 2 black print and 2 black plaid straps.

Stitch one black print piece to a black plaid one as shown. Repeat.

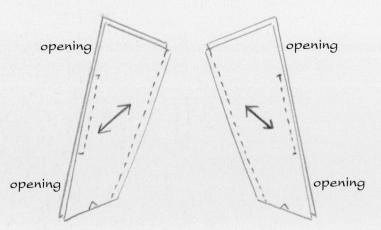

Trim away excess seam allowance and turn right side out. Press.

Stitch the back straps to the side of the vest bodice, matching seams and colors with right sides together. Press seams toward the bodice. Slipstitch the opening to close.

Stitch neck straps to the top of the vest bodice the same way, matching seams, notches, and colors. Press seams toward the bodice. Slipstitch the opening to close.

Stitch the center back seams on neck straps together. Press seams open. Slipstitch the opening closed.

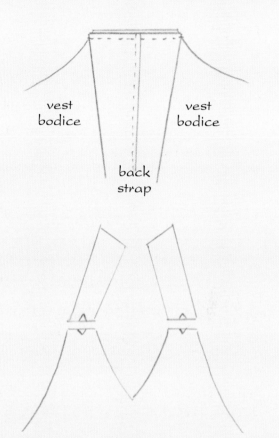

PHOTO: Wooil Kim

PHOTO: Wooil Kim

Mellifluence Apron Vest

Courthouse Steps Piecing

Cut 1" strips in 3 different red print fabrics (red A, red B, red C), 2 different black print fabrics (black D, black E), and one ivory fabric.

Make a strip-set as shown. Press seams toward the black strips.

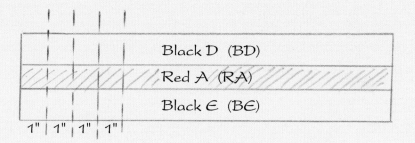

Cut the strip-set into 1" segments (piece 1).

Chain stitch all piece 1 segments to a red B strip as shown. Cut between pieces (piece 2). Press seams toward red B strips.

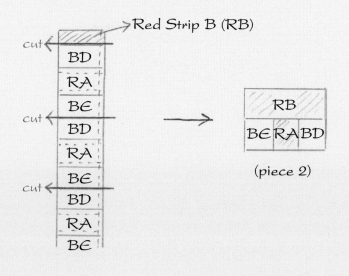

Chain stitch the opposite side of piece 2 to an ivory strip. Cut between pieces (piece 3) and press seams toward the ivory strip.

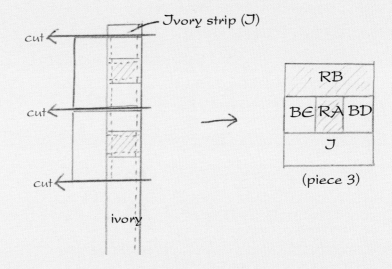

(piece 3)

Chain stitch piece 3 to a black D strip as shown. Cut between pieces (piece 4) and press seams toward the black D strip.

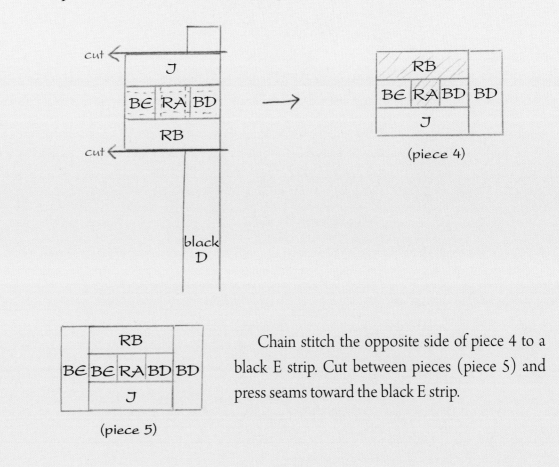

(piece 4)

(piece 5)

Chain stitch the opposite side of piece 4 to a black E strip. Cut between pieces (piece 5) and press seams toward the black E strip.

Continue in this manner, chain stitching the opposite side of the pieces to a red, then an ivory strip, then chain stitching the other two sides alternately to the black D and E strips until there are 3 "steps" of each fabric as shown.

Join the blocks as shown to create the Courthouse Steps fabric.

			RC			
			RC			
			RB			
BE	BE	BE	RA	BD	BD	BD
			J			
			J			
			J			

complete block

Trace the apron vest pattern (on CD) onto pattern paper.

whole vest
paper pattern piece

Draw in the design lines following the diagram, arranging and changing them as you wish.

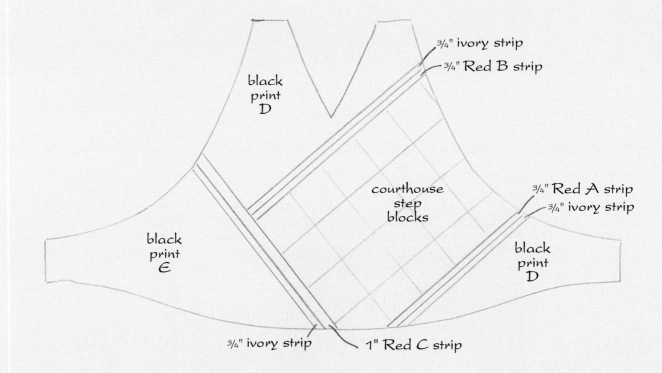

Trace each section onto tracing paper. Cut them out and use as templates.

Place each paper template on the right side of the fabric indicated. Cut out the sections, adding ¼" seam allowance where they will be seamed and 1" along the outside edges. (See pages 71–72 for examples of adding the extra allowance.)

Join the sections as shown in the drawing above. Use the pattern as a guide and trim off the excess.

Use the MELLIFLUENCE vest as a lining for the Resonance vest OR cut a plain lining and join according to the instructions on page 79.

Resonance & Mellifluence

Matching Pouch Bag

Making the
Matching Pouch Bag

Cut 3" x 17" strips and piece together following the same procedure as for the RESONANCE apron vest (pages 77–78). I used 4 different fabrics.

Stitch ¼" tucks for the bag (⅛" tucks were made for the vest). The front and back should measure 16½" x 17".

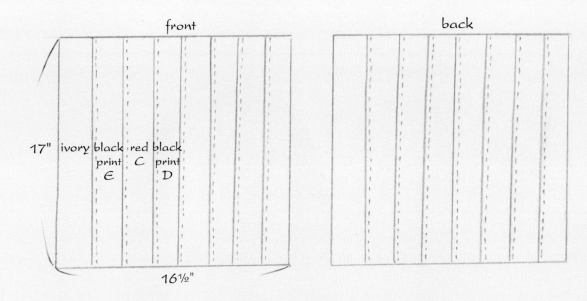

front

back

17" | ivory | black print E | red C | black print D

16½"

Cut 2 pieces of batting 17½" x 18".

Layer each piece with batting and pin the layers together.

Mark horizontal lines 2" apart and stitch across the tucks in alternating directions as shown. Use a walking foot when stitching.

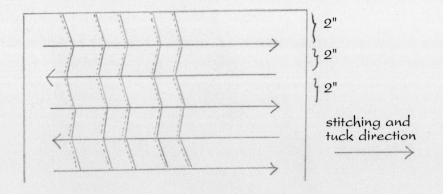

} 2"

} 2"

} 2"

stitching and tuck direction

Gently steam press both pieces. Do not move the iron back and forth.

Using the bag pattern, cut out a front and back.

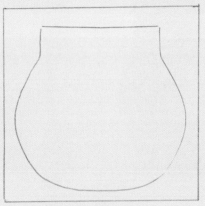

1 front & 1 back

Stitch front and back pieces with right sides together using a ½" seam allowance, leaving an opening at the top. Clip inward curves and trim away excess seam allowances. Turn right side out and press.

Cut out a lining using the same pattern piece. Add inside pockets if you wish.

Join the front and back lining pieces leaving an opening at both the top and bottom.

Place outside pouch into the lining with right sides together. Pin the top opening together and stitch all the way around. Turn right side out through the bottom opening of the lining. Slip-stitch the opening closed.

Press the top edge and topstitch ⅛" from the edge. Install handles of your choice.

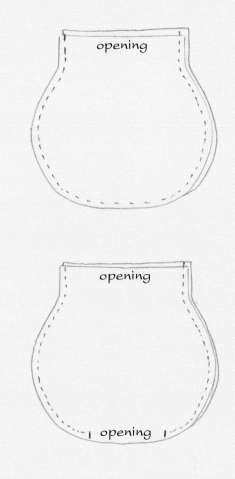

Technique E:
3-D Folded Square

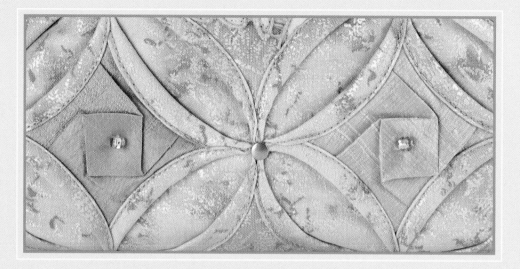

Determine the size of your finished square and add ½" seam allowance. For example, for a finished square 1¾" x 1¾", cut 2¼" x 2¼" square.

Cut a muslin square the unfinished size (2¼" x 2¼") as a base and a fashion fabric square 1" larger (3¼" x 3¼").

Fold the fashion fabric square in half, wrong sides together. Pinch both edges along the fold to make ½" long creases. Unfold and refold to make ½" long creases on the other two sides.

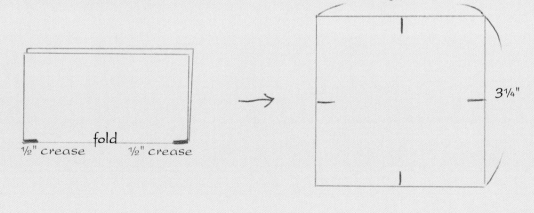

Place the larger square on the muslin square, wrong sides together. Pin each corner of the larger square to its corresponding corner on the small muslin square.

Pinch the fabric at a crease to make a pleat to the right of the pinch and pin to the small square. Repeat on all four sides.

To form a square-on-point in the middle, rotate and pat down the center at the same time.

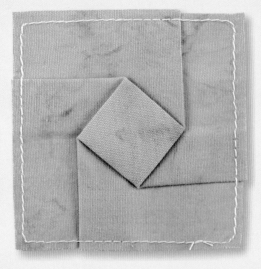

Press gently with an iron.

Remove the muslin square while maintaining the tucks and folds and machine baste ⅛" from the edge all the way around.

After mounting the square on a background, add a seed bead in the center or at the four corners of the square-on-point of your 3-D folded square.

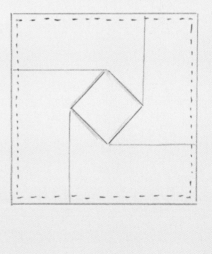

Imperial
Jacket & Bag

Jiyoung Yun

Imperial

Jacket & Bag

This jacket is created solely from Cathedral Window blocks, which originated from Korean wrapping cloth called *Bojahgy*. To create this updated imperial look of Korean royal queens, you do not need to have any pattern at all.

Approximate Fabric Requirements

7–8 yards fashion fabric

Notions

iron-on brass tacks, crystals, or beads
handles, 2 buttons, and snap fastener

Calculating the Size of Squares

Calculate the size of your Cathedral Window blocks depending on your bust measurement and the desired amount of ease.

Measure your bust in inches (for example, 38").

Add ease of 4"–6".
For a more fitted jacket add 4" (38 + 4 = 42").
For a semi-loose fitting jacket add 6" (38 + 6 = 44").

Let's say we decided on a fitted jacket. Divide 42 by 4. Let's call this number **A**.
$42 \div 4 = 10\frac{1}{2}"$

Then divide A by 3. Let's call this number **B**.
$10\frac{1}{2}" \div 3 = 3\frac{1}{2}"$

The cutting size of your squares will be
$2 \times B + \frac{1}{2}"$ seam allowance.
$2 \times 3\frac{1}{2}" + \frac{1}{2}" = 7\frac{1}{2}"$ squares

Choosing Fabrics

For Cathedral Window blocks it is better to use lightweight fabrics such as silk dupioni, lightweight cotton eyelet (see the SHERBET jacket, pages 105–107), or lightweight batik cotton since you are going to have 4 layers of fabric when the background squares are folded to form windows.

Preparing Background Cathedral Window Blocks

Cut squares of the calculated measurement for your size.

Fold squares in half, right sides together, and stitch each end with a ¼" seam. If you use silk dupioni squares, stitch the crosswise grain sides first since they tend to ravel more.

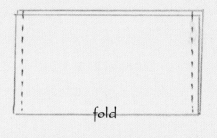

fold

Pull the open edges of the folded square and re-fold with the seam lines matching. Stitch from each corner to within 1" of the center opening. Trim the corner seam allowances at a 45-degree angle.

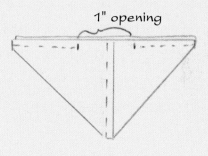

1" opening

Press the seams open and turn the folded square right sides out through the opening and press again.

Bring each corner to the center of the seamed side and press firmly. Do not move the iron back and forth.

Secure the 4 corners at the center with a tiny cross-stitch through all layers.

Joining the Background Blocks

Join background blocks with narrow zigzag stitches. Start with a narrow stitch width and a stitch length of 0 to tack the ends. Once tacked, increase the stitch length and zigzag along the 2 folded edges. At the end, decrease length setting to 0 to tack the ends again.

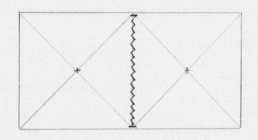

Join squares for the bodice, back, and sleeves as shown. Add quilting stitches through all layers as follows:

Front, 21 squares in a 3 x 7 arrangement; make 2

Back, 42 squares in a 6 x 7 arrangement

Sleeves, 30 squares in a 6 x 5 arrangement; make 2

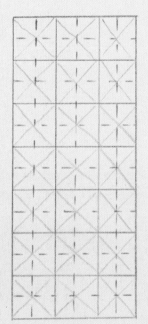

Embellishing the Windows

Add lace motifs and free-motion topstitch them in place. Fold back the surrounding block edges into a curve and topstitch in place.

To make 3-D folded square insets for the windows, measure the size of your background window square. For example, 2½" x 2½".

To make 3-D folded square insets for the windows, measure the size of your background window square. For example, 2½" x 2½".

Cut a muslin square ¼" smaller (2¼" x 2 ¼") as a base and a fashion fabric square 1" larger (3¼" x 3¼").

Follow the Technique E instructions (pages 90–91).

Place and pin the 3-D folded square over the zigzag seam joining two Cathedral Window blocks as shown.

Beginning in one corner, roll the surrounding border over the edge of the 3-D folded square, stretching this curve down to secure the square. Topstitch with matching color thread. Add iron-on or stitched embellishments if desired.

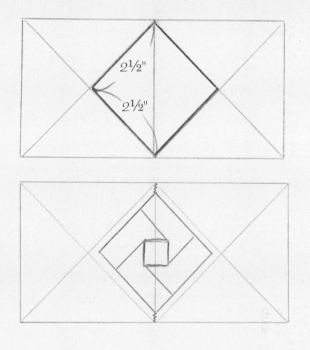

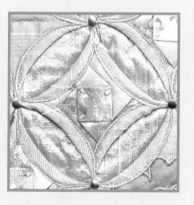

Assembling the Jacket

Join the shoulder seams by zigzag stitching the two outside blocks as shown.

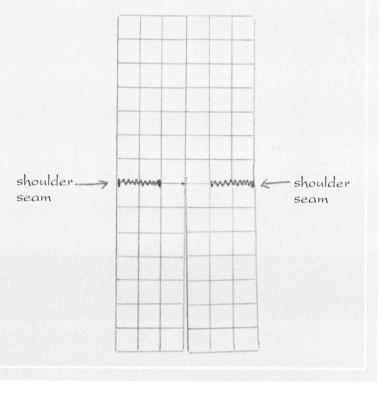

shoulder seam → ⟵ shoulder seam

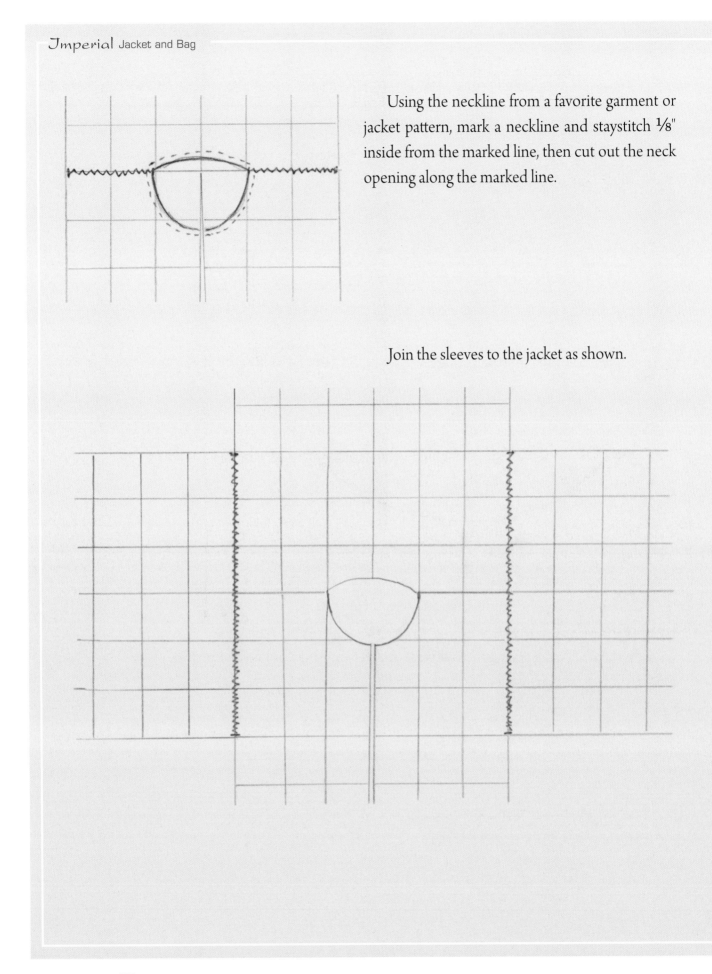

Using the neckline from a favorite garment or jacket pattern, mark a neckline and staystitch ⅛" inside from the marked line, then cut out the neck opening along the marked line.

Join the sleeves to the jacket as shown.

Slipstitch the underarm and side seams by hand.

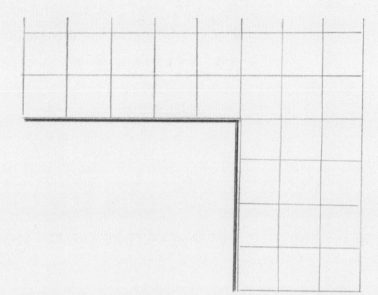

Prepare 2¼" wide bias strips to bind the edges of the jacket. The sample jacket used approximately 110" of binding.

Fold the strips in half lengthwise, wrong sides together, and press. Stitch ¼" from the edges, turn to the back, and hand finish.

Finishing the Sleeves

Measure the distance around your wrist to determine the finished width of the sleeve (for example, medium size width is 11").

Use a double strand of matching thread and hand stitch running stitches on the edge of the sleeves. Gather to the desired measurement.

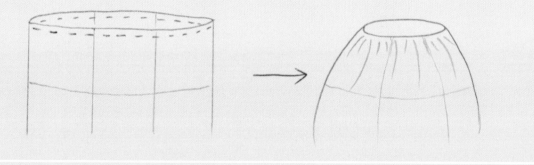

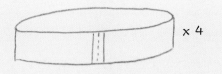

four sleeve belts

× 4

Cut four 2" strips the jacket wrist width + 1" (11 + 1 = 12"). With right sides together, stitch each strip at the shorter ends with a ½" seam allowance to form a tube. Press the seams open.

For the ruffle, cut two 5" wide bias strips, double the sleeve width + 1" (2 x 11 + 1 = 23"). With right sides together, stitch each bias strip at the shorter ends with a ½" seam allowance to form 2 tubes for the sleeve belts. Press seams open.

5"   5"

With wrong sides together, fold the bias strip tubes in half lengthwise.

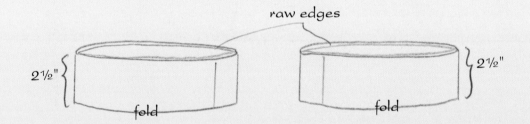

raw edges

2½"   2½"

fold   fold

At the raw edges, machine baste 2 rows of stitches, ⅛" and ⅜" from the edges. Pull the bobbin thread ends, gathering the ruffle to fit the sleeve belts.

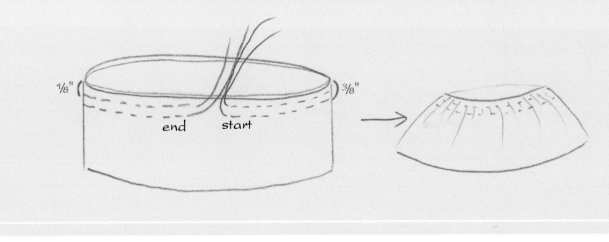

⅛"   ⅜"

end   start

Sandwich each gathered ruffle between two sleeve belts and stitch ¼" from the raw edges. Press seams toward sleeve belts. Remove the basting threads.

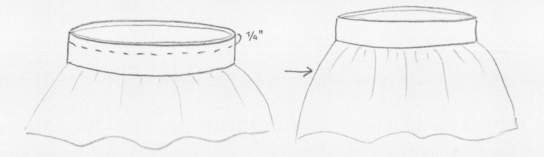

Fold under ¼" on the inside sleeve belts.

Stitch the outside sleeve belt to the gathered sleeve with a ¼" seam. Press seams toward the sleeve belt. Slipstitch the folded inside sleeve belt to the sleeve.

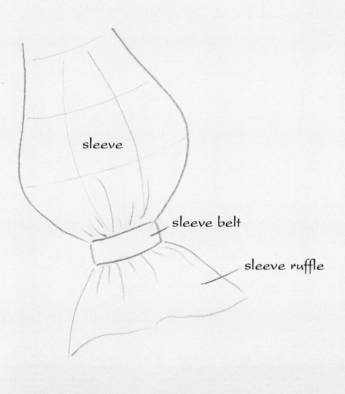

Imperial Bag

Cut 50 squares 7½" x 7½" for a large bag and 7" x 7" for a medium-size bag.

Prepare 50 background Cathedral Window blocks and join 25 blocks for the front and the other 25 for the back in a 5 x 5 arrangement.

Embellish by inserting 3-D folded squares and topstitching lace motifs as you did for the jacket. Beginning in one corner, roll the surrounding border over the edge, stretching the bias edge to create a curve. Stitch this curve down onto the square with matching thread and a short straight stitch. Add a seed bead to the center of the 3-D folded squares.

Join one side seam using zigzag stitches.

Join the bottom using zigzag stitches and hand stitches as shown.

Lastly hand slipstitch or whipstitch the last side seam.

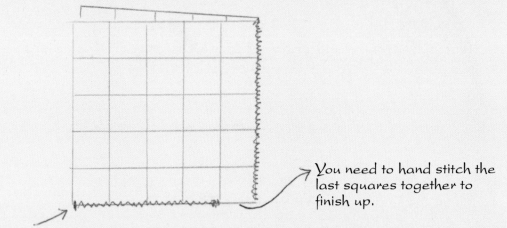

You need to hand stitch the last squares together to finish up.

Start from this point and zigzag stitch as far as you can.

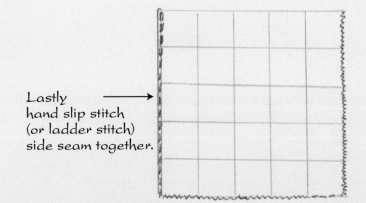

Lastly hand slip stitch (or ladder stitch) side seam together.

You do not need to line this bag. Install handles of your choice. To get a flat bottom, stitch two buttons on sides to hold up pointed ends. Tuck in the top ends and add a snap fastener in line with the handles to shape the bag.

PHOTO: Wooil Kim

Sherbet

Jacket Variation

Approximate Fabric Requirements

7–8 yards lightweight cotton eyelet
assorted scraps in sherbet colors
½ yard cotton for neckline binding

Notions

1–1½ yards 3"–4" wide white eyelet ribbon
trim

Follow the square calculations (page 94) and instructions (pages 95–101) as for the IMPERIAL jacket.

For the ruffled collar, staystitch and trim off the front necklines using the vest pattern front neckline (see CD).

Stitch collar sections together at the center back using a ½" seam allowance. Press seams open. Repeat.

Stitch the front and back collar together at the outer edge using ½" seam allowance. Trim seam allowance ¼".

Turn right side out. Press. Baste the raw edges together.

Make pleats on the inside of the collar, bringing 2 pleat lines together as shown. Baste and stitch.

On the outside, flatten the pleat at the center and press. Baste close to the folds and across the upper edge. Press.

Pin the collar to the jacket neckline, clipping the neck edge where necessary.

Finish with matching double-fold bias binding.

Measure the width of the sleeve edge. Cut a length of the eyelet trim twice that measurement.

Join with a ½" seam allowance and press the seam open.

Gather along one edge and pin to the sleeve edge, right sides together, adjusting the gathers as necessary to fit. Stitch in place.

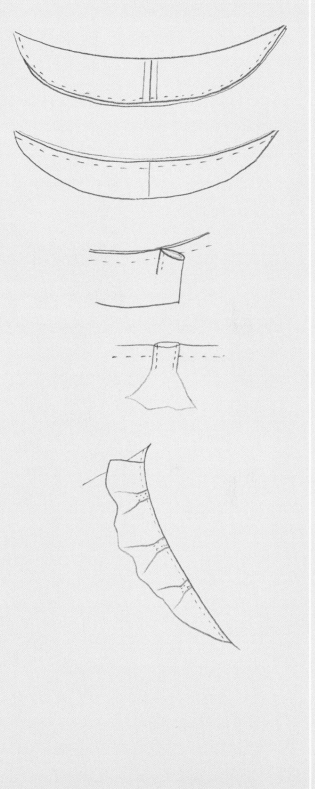

Design Ideas
Allure Jacket
Eclectic Jacket (opposite)

Jiyoung Yun

PHOTO: Wooil Kim

PHOTO: Wooil Kim

Resources

Visit the author's Web site for additional patterns and purse handles.
www.ramikim.com

Bernina USA
www.berninausa.com

Britex Fabrics
146 Geary Street
San Francisco, CA 94108
Phone: 415-392-2910
Web site: **www.britexfabrics.com**
  For fabrics, buttons, lace motifs, and decorative braids

Ghee's
PO Box 4424
Shreveport, LA 71134
Phone: 318-226-1701
E-mail: **bags@ghees.com**
Web site: **www.ghees.com**
  For handbag supplies and zippers

J. R. Flamingo Fabrics
1139 Fulton Ave, Suite C
Sacramento, CA 95825
Phone: 916-481-1139
Web site: **www.jrflamingo.com**
  For silk dupioni and other fabrics

WEBS®
75 Service Center Road
Northampton, MA 01060
Phone: 800-367-9327
Web site: **www.yarn.com**
  For the Blocking Board, a gridded, padded working surface in two sizes (18" x 24" and 33" x 51")

LEFT: *Decorative pillow, another design idea*

About the Author

Rami Kim started sewing making Barbie® doll clothes for her two daughters, Deanna and Chelsey (now two bright teenagers, 18 and 15 years old). As a former scientist, creating micro-garments fascinated her imagination.

Later she happened to take a free strip-piecing quilting class at a local fabric store. It was a beautiful beginning to her new career as a fabric artist.

Since then, she has won 13 Best of Show awards for her art-to-wear garments and accumulated nine sewing machines (and sold some!).

She travels nationally and internationally to do lectures and workshops and is recognized everywhere for her outstanding designs and meticulous workmanship.

This is Rami's second book. *Folded Fabric Elegance* was published by AQS in 2007.

PHOTO: Wooil Kim